CONTENTS

DENISE LEE YOHN
brand-building expert | speaker | author

INTRODUCTION
ARE YOU READY TO SCALE-UP YOUR BRAND?

Breaking up may be the hardest thing to do in relationships, but scaling up is definitely the hardest thing to do in business. Some estimate that nine out of 10 start-ups fail.

If you want to be among the few that survive and thrive, you must have a solid strategic brand platform in place. With this in mind, I've developed this workbook, *Scale-Up Your Brand.*

WHY DO THIS?

There are lots of start-ups, but many fewer scale-ups. Companies often don't make the leap between the two because of their brand strategy -- or lack thereof. They get lost on the path that Yogi Berra described when he observed, "If you don't know where you're going, you'll end up someplace else."

A clear, focused, and robust strategic brand platform can serve as a compass and guide to help you navigate the millions of difficult decisions about what to do and how to do it that you will face as you grow.

By using this workbook, you will develop the strategic brand platform your growing organization needs. You will:

- Lay the foundation for your brand to inspire true customer loyalty, improve your profit margin, and increase the longevity of your business
- Specify how you plan to compete and win
- Achieve clarity, focus, and alignment on your priorities among everyone who works on your business

THE FIVE STEPS

In this workbook I lay out the five steps I take with clients who are looking to grow from a small business into a larger enterprise or from later-stage start-up to IPO ready.

 Step 1: Conduct a Brand Diagnostic -- Start with a diagnostic evaluation of your brand to assess its current strength and to identify opportunities for brand-building and growth.

 Step 2: Set Your Brand Purpose, Values, and Defining Attributes -- Clearly articulate your brand's reason for being, the principles that guide your way of doing things, and the operating characteristics and personality traits that distinguish your brand.

 Step 3: Identify Your Core Customer Target -- Specify the primary type of person or group of people you want as customers.

 Step 4: Plot Your Brand Position -- Identify the optimal position for your brand in the competitive landscape.

 Step 5: Determine Your Key Differentiators -- Indicate the features, aspects, and benefits of your product or service that set it apart the most from competing brands.

 Bonus: Assess Your Brand Power -- Evaluate your brand strategy on five critical dimensions.

Together these steps provide a roadmap to developing a strong, valuable, sustainable brand strategy that will help you scale.

WORK AS A TEAM

I recommend you form a team of 3-6 people to work through these exercises together. Include key brand stakeholders — i.e., people who have a key stake in the success of your brand — such as the founders, key executives, critical employees, investors, strategic partners, and perhaps even a select customer or two. Sometimes it's helpful to include an objective facilitator to encourage open and active participation and/or an inspirational muse to contribute out-of-the box ideas.

The goal is to get everyone's insights and input on the brand out on the table and to develop a clear shared vision for the brand. The process of doing the exercises together creates one common understanding and ensures that different perspectives are considered in the development of the brand platform.

List your brand team members

One final note: These exercises are simply tools to cultivate robust discussion. If you find your group deviating from the exercise process but having an illuminating discussion about the brand anyway, go with the flow — you'll likely end up in the same place. Likewise, don't just go through the motion of the exercises without ensuring that they prompt productive conversation and point you toward definitive conclusions.

LET'S GET STARTED!

DENISE LEE YOHN
brand-building expert | speaker | author

STEP 1: CONDUCT A BRAND DIAGNOSTIC

Every successful journey starts with a sober and thorough examination of where you're starting from. This chapter lays out the first step in your scaling journey. You'll learn how to conduct a Brand Diagnostic, a diagnostic evaluation of your brand to assess its current strength and to identify opportunities for brand-building and growth.

A Brand Diagnostic involves two exercises:

A. Audit and Analysis -- auditing and analyzing your brand through three critical lenses

B. Objective-Driven S.W.O.T. -- determining your essential strengths, weaknesses, opportunities, and threats

EXERCISE A: AUDIT AND ANALYSIS

Examine your brand from three perspectives:

1 **Customers.** Understand who are your current and prospective customers and assess perceptions of your brand among those who are your most ideal customers — the people who are most likely to become your most loyal, profitable customers.

- Assess how customers can be segmented into distinct and meaningful groupings; then determine which ones are the best fit with your brand and how well you are acquiring and retaining those.
- Identify your primary segments' needs, wants, usage occasions, and drivers of purchase and re-purchase.
- Determine how your brand is perceived on these dimensions.

  Use industry data, your own market research, and even social listening to glean these insights. If you have a lot of data and sophisticated research and analytics capabilities, your findings will be very specific and projectable; if you don't, use whatever information you have to make educated hypotheses that you can validate in the future.

Note the key conclusions from your Customer Audit & Analysis here:

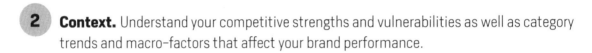

....

....

....

....

....

....

....

....

....

---

2 **Context.** Understand your competitive strengths and vulnerabilities as well as category trends and macro-factors that affect your brand performance.

- Use your target customers' consideration sets to identify your primary direct and indirect competitors; then assess how your brand compares to them on your customers' decision-making criteria, e.g., price, quality, convenience, etc.

- Identify key trends in your category such as technological developments and emerging competitors and determine how they might impact your brand performance.

- Identify macro environmental factors such as the economic climate, cultural influences, and social trends and determine how they impact your brand perceptions.

Again, the depth and scope of your analysis depends on the amount and type of data you have access to, but most of this information is available through Internet searches, trend reports, and media audits.

Note the key conclusions from your Context Audit & Analysis here:

---

3 **Company.** Understand the current state of your brand, your business, and your organization.

- Evaluate your existing products/services and those in your pipeline in terms of perceived value, differentiation, and long-term viability.

- Assess your current capabilities, assets, and resources (human, financial, etc.) and identify underleveraged ones.

- Evaluate your current brand strategy (if you have one) and how it is used — is it clear, focused, and differentiating? Do all stakeholders share one common understanding of it? Is it operationalized throughout your organization?

You can learn most of what you need to know here through organizational self-assessments, interviews/surveys among key external stakeholders, and internal audits. See Bonus tool on Page 29 for one approach to evaluating your brand.

> **Note the key conclusions from your Company Audit & Analysis here:**
>
> ....
>
> ....
>
> ....
>
> ....
>
> ....
>
> ....
>
> ....

EXERCISE B: OBJECTIVE-DRIVEN S.W.O.T.

Conduct a S.W.O.T. analysis based on the learnings from the first exercise.

Keep in mind a singular objective -- e.g., achieving a leadership position in your industry, offering an attractive investment opportunity, etc. -- as you do this exercise.

Organize your points into four categories:

Strengths: What are your inherent strengths that have been or can be instrumental in achieving the objective?

Weaknesses: What are your inherent weaknesses that have or will hold you back from achieving the objective?

Opportunities: What new opportunities should you seize to increase the likelihood of achieving the objective?

Threats: What is out of your control that could jeopardize your ability to achieve the objective?

Start by listing as many points as possible and then prioritize the top 3-5 in each category.

S.W.O.T.

OBJECTIVE: ....

STRENGTHS

WEAKNESSES

OPPORTUNITIES

THREATS

The outcomes of your S.W.O.T. serve as a diagnosis of your brand today, giving you clarity on what needs to improve and what can be leveraged and exploited. It will also point to new growth opportunities for you to explore.

A Brand Diagnostic is the first step in your scale-up journey. Now, on to setting your Brand Purpose, Values, and Defining Attributes!

DENISE LEE YOHN
brand-building expert | speaker | author

STEP 2: SET YOUR BRAND PURPOSE, VALUES, AND DEFINING ATTRIBUTES

In this step of scaling up your brand, you'll learn how to flesh out the core elements of your strategic brand platform.

WHAT IS A STRATEGIC BRAND PLATFORM?

Let's begin with some definitions:

- **Brand purpose** is your brand's reason for being/what your brand stands for

- **Key brand values** are the principles that guide your brand's actions -- in other words, your brand's unique way of doing things

- **Defining brand attributes** are the operating characteristics and personality traits that distinguish your brand

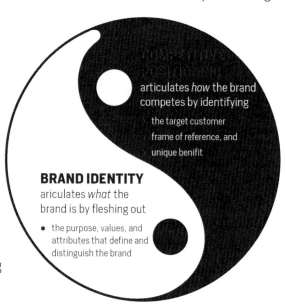

COMPETITIVE POSITIONING articulates *how* the brand competes by identifying

the target customer frame of reference, and unique benifit

BRAND IDENTITY ariculates *what* the brand is by fleshing out

- the purpose, values, and attributes that define and distinguish the brand

Strategic Brand Platform

These three elements comprise your Brand Identity, which is one half of the strategic platform of your brand. Your Competitive Brand Positioning is the other half of your strategic brand platform. Together they form the building blocks that create a strong, differentiated, valuable brand. (Learn more about Strategic Brand Platforms and why you need one here: **http://deniseleeyohn.com/bites/strategic-brand-platforms/**).

CRAFT YOUR STRATEGIC BRAND PLATFORM

Exercises like the ones in this workbook are helpful in developing these brand building blocks because they cause you and other participants to be thoughtful and deliberate about the brand you're creating and why — and they help you be more articulate and specific as you describe your brand vision.

Ultimately your strategic brand platform serves as a roadmap on your growth journey. It helps you and everyone in your organization to determine what to say "yes" and "no" to.

We'll start with exercises that will help you develop your Brand Identity. You'll work on your Competitive Brand Positioning in Steps 3 – 5.

EXERCISE 1: THINK. FEEL. DO.

The first exercise is a Thematic Apperception "Test" (TAT) borrowed from the field of psychology. It's a projective exercise, meaning that it helps to reveal underlying motives, appeals, and concerns. Most TATs use ambiguous pictures of people and ask participants to make up narratives about the images. We will use a TAT to help uncover your brand's purpose and values.

- Use before and after stick figure pictures of a customer.
- Ask participants to create two sets of narratives about the customer's thoughts, feelings, and actions -- one that happens before he is aware of your brand; the second, after he becomes aware of your brand and tries it. Specifically:
  - **Think:** what is he thinking about the choices he has; what is going through his mind as he considers where to go/what to buy
  - **Feel:** what is he feeling about the decision he is going to make; what emotions does he experience as he goes to buy the product
  - **Do:** what does he do; what decision does he make
- Look for similarities and differences among the narratives created by the different participants. Discuss the appeal of the similarities and the reasons for the differences.
- Extract from the discussion key themes that form your brand purpose and values. Consider articulating your brand purpose with the phrase "We exist to..." and your brand values with the phrase "We believe..." You will continue to work on your brand values as you move onto the next exercise.

Think. Feel. Do. Worksheet

💡 TIPS:

- As a warm-up or to get unstuck, ask participants to do a version of this exercise for their favorite brand.

- Even though this should be a fun and creative process and the use of stick figures in this exercise specifically may seem playful, encourage participants to think deeply as they create the narratives. You may have to ask them to re-do their TAT a few times as they unpeel the onion of possible answers.

- You really want to get at the change in the world you see your brand making and how your brand makes it. For example, in the post-launch "Do" section, get beyond the basic outcome that customers will go buy the brand once it's available. Consider how your brand might change their lives — how they might relate to themselves, people, and/or their environments differently because of your brand; or what decisions they might make differently; how they might spend their time or money differently.

- To push the group's thinking, consider asking everyone to select a brand that they want your brand to emulate and have everyone write narratives about it — then discuss how the themes relate to your brand.

DENISE LEE YOHN
brand-building expert | speaker | author

EXERCISE 2: IS/IS NOT

The second exercise uses an adjective checklist to identify the core values, operating characteristics, and personality traits that define the way your brand behaves and that distinguish your brand.

- Develop a list of 50-75 descriptive adjectives to give to each participant. The effectiveness of this exercise depends on the quality of the list. [See the example on the next page of a list I used for a new brand of healthful snacks.] Select words that:
  - ✓ Are different from ones that describe your primary competitors and the category in general. Delicious is not a helpful descriptor for a food brand, for example, so don't include it.
  - ✓ Help to parse out nuanced but important ideas. For example, comfortable, down-to-earth, and laid-back are similar terms but each connotes a slightly different feel, so you might include all of them if you want to get clarity on the dimension.
  - ✓ Are drivers that reflect customers' unmet and unfelt needs. If you think customers are looking for, say, some excitement in your category, you might include words like exciting, stimulating, or refreshing.
  - ✓ You have previously heard stakeholders use to describe the brand.

- Ask each participant to circle up to five adjectives that describe what your brand IS and cross out up to five adjectives that it IS NOT.

- Give them the option of writing in their own words, but they should do so only if they believe an important factor is not represented by any of the words on the page. Their write-ins should be single-word, descriptive adjectives.

- As with Exercise #1, look for similarities and differences among people's choices. Discuss the relevance of the similarities and the subtleties of the differences.

- Extract from the discussion the descriptors that make up your core brand values and the defining attributes of your brand. Narrow the list down to 3-5 of each. Consider articulating your brand values with the phrase "We believe..." and your brand attributes with the phrase "We are..." Also create short descriptors for each value and attribute so that their meaning is clear.

IS/IS NOT

Circle up to 5 adjectives that describe what the brand IS; X up to 5 adjectives that it IS NOT.

- accepting
- active
- bold
- calm
- caring
- centered
- challenging
- charismatic
- charming
- comfortable
- conservative
- courageous
- creative
- detail-oriented
- distinctive
- down-to-earth
- dynamic
- earthy
- elegant

- encouraging
- energetic
- entertaining
- exciting
- fashionable
- first class
- fresh
- friendly
- funny
- helpful
- hip
- imaginative
- in the know
- indulgent
- ingenious
- inspirational
- intimate
- intuitive
- joyful

- laid-back
- leader
- liberating
- maternal
- modern
- normal
- nurturing
- old-fashioned
- open
- personal
- positive
- powerful
- practical
- quiet
- quirky
- real
- reliable
- safe
- savvy

- sensual
- sensitive
- serious
- sophisticated
- straightforward
- strong
- supportive
- surprising
- thoughtful
- traditional
- trend-setting
- trustworthy
- up-to-date
- worm
- wholesome
- youthful
- other:
- other:
- other:

Sample List for IS/IS NOT Exercise

 TIPS:

- Ask participants to select the words that describe your brand when it's at its best. This will help you identify values and attributes that are as positive as possible while being realistic.

- Avoid words like "authentic" and "cool" since these descriptors fall into the "if you have to say it, you're not" category.

- Don't include "fun" or "passionate" because every brand aspires to these descriptors -- unless the degree to or nature with which your brand would embrace these ideas is particularly distinguishing.

With these two exercises, you should be able to articulate a first draft of your brand purpose, values, and defining attributes. You might want to revisit these elements as you work through the rest of your strategic brand platform, but for now, put together your Brand Identity.

BRAND IDENTITY

Write in the elements of your Brand Identity here:

Brand Purpose: We exist to:

Brand Values: We believe:

Brand Defining Attributes: We are:

With the elements of your Brand Identity set, you're ready to start working on your Brand Positioning strategy.

DENISE LEE YOHN
brand-building expert | speaker | author

STEP 3: IDENTIFY YOUR CORE CUSTOMER TARGET

A clear Competitive Brand Positioning strategy is the next step to scale-up your brand. A Competitive Brand Positioning is essential to brand-building because it defines who you are selling to, what your business scope is, and how you create unique value for customers. Before we get into identifying the optimal position for your brand, we need to discuss brand positioning in general.

WHAT IS BRAND POSITIONING?

As noted previously, your Competitive Brand Positioning is the other part of the strategic platform for your brand. It describes how you compare and compete with other brands. While your Brand Identity should be evergreen, your Competitive Brand Positioning will change as your customers and context change. (Learn more about brand positioning in this post: ***http://deniseleeyohn.com/bites/competitive-brand-positioning/*** and in Chapter Three of my book, ***What Great Brands Do***.)

You might have an intuitive understanding of your competitive strategy, but it's important to take the time to flesh out and clearly articulate your Competitive Brand Positioning in a strategic statement.

A Competitive Brand Positioning statement uses this framework:

> For [core customer], we are the [competitive frame of reference] who does [unique value], because [reason(s) to believe].

WHO DO YOU WANT AT YOUR CORE?

The first [blank] to fill in is your core customer target -- that is, the type of person or group of people that you want as customers. You can't be all things to all people, so specifying your core customer target helps you prioritize your efforts and focus your resources on those people who are going to be your most loyal and profitable ones.

More established, resourced organizations should identify their core customer target by undertaking needs-based segmentation research which involves using quantitative survey data and multivariate analysis to cluster customers into needs-based segments of different value by combining their attitudes and usage occasions. (Learn more about needs-based segmentation here ***http://deniseleeyohn.com/bites/catering-to-shoppers-need-states/*** and in Chapter Four of my book, ***What Great Brands Do***.)

Start-ups and scale-ups can usually use the following less data-based, more creative and simpler approach.

DEVELOP A MEANINGFUL PROFILE

You probably already have a sense of your core customers' demographics (e.g., adults aged 18-54) and category behaviors (what they currently buy, where they shop, what products/brands they use). You might even know you want to target customers of a certain economic value (e.g., customers who spend $500+ in our category, companies that have more than 100 employees, etc.)

Your strategic brand platform should describe your core customers with more distinguishing, meaningful characteristics -- their values, attitudes, needs, goals. Sometimes it is difficult to get at these descriptors without some stimuli -- other times, you might be struggling to achieve consensus about your target among different stakeholders. One exercise to help you arrive at a clear, common understanding of your target is to create a Customer Collage.

EXERCISE: CUSTOMER COLLAGE

- Collect a bunch of magazines for the team. Select the magazines carefully. Use titles that are relevant but not necessarily in your category (e.g., if you're working on a healthy food brand, select fitness/exercise magazines or titles having to do with gardening or homemaking.)
- Ask each participant to:
    - cut out at least six images that portray your core customer target
    - assemble their images into a collage with glue or tape
    - give their collage a "title" that captures the essence and core descriptors of the target
- Once everyone is finished, ask each person to present their collage to the team, explaining why they chose the images and title. Create a list of the words and ideas that they use.

- Discuss the list of descriptors as a team, analyzing, synthesizing, and prioritizing them to create a succinct description or short set of bullet points that describe your core customer target.

 TIPS:

- If you have a large group, get multiple copies of the same magazines, so that more than one person can use the same image if they desire.

- Remind participants that the images shouldn't just represent the target's demographics -- they should relate to their attitudes, lifestyles, values, and drivers.

- Ask people to talk about what images they deliberately did *not* include in their collage and to describe images they were looking for but couldn't find, and why. Their explanations of these can be as illuminating as their descriptions of their collages.

CORE CUSTOMER TARGET

Write in your core customer Target description here:

....

....

....

....

After identifying your core customer target, you can move on to the rest of your Brand Positioning.

STEP 4: PLOT YOUR BRAND POSITION

In this step, you'll learn how to identify the optimal position for your brand in the competitive landscape.

Remember the Competitive Brand Positioning statement framework is:

> For [core customer], we are the [competitive frame of reference] who does [unique value], because [reason(s) to believe].

The following process refers to the second and third [blanks]: your competitive frame of reference (or category of choice) and your unique value (or unique customer benefit).

UNDERSTAND THE TERMS

Your competitive frame of reference is the "mental file folder" you want your customers to put your brand in. Usually this is your industry category, but keep in mind that people don't necessarily think of products in terms of specific categories, and in some cases you might be creating a new category, so your frame of reference may not be obvious.

Plus, many purchase decisions involve "indirect competition" in which consumers ask themselves: Juice or soda? Dinner or movie? Vacation or new car? So your competitive frame of reference requires careful consideration.

The unique value of your brand is what you do for people that no one does as well as you, or no one else does at all. You should think about and articulate this in terms of a customer benefit, i.e., what's in it for them. Look at the value you create from your customers' -- not your own -- point of view.

Your unique value will differ depending on your competitive frame of reference so you should develop these two elements simultaneously.

FIVE PARTS OF THE BRAND POSITIONING DEVELOPMENT PROCESS

Follow this process to define your competitive frame of reference and identify your unique value:

1 **Think big.**

Start by thinking broadly about what business you're really in.

- Consider what you do for people instead of the product/service you produce or sell. You might be selling running shoes, but are you really in the healthy living business? You may be a mobile carrier, but are you really in the productivity business? You might be an insurance provider, but are you really in the freedom business?

- Create a list of the possible businesses you might be in and put them in order from the narrowest to the broadest.

2 **Consider lifestage.**

Consider what lifestage your brand or product is in.

- If you are just starting out, you should define your competitive frame of reference more narrowly since your primary challenge is simply getting people to choose you over other existing options. Later in the lifestage of your product or brand, you should define your frame more broadly since you'll probably want to consider avenues for new growth through adjacent markets, categories, and capabilities.

- Review your list from #1 and determine the best business scope for your competitive frame of reference given your lifestage.

COMPETITIVE FRAME OF REFERENCE OPTIONS

1. Fill in the list of possible businesses you might be in:

....

....

....

....

2. Place a star next to the one that seems the best frame of reference

---

DENISE LEE YOHN
brand-building expert | speaker | author

3 **Identify competitors.**

List the major competitive brands in your frame of reference and identify the unique value that each delivers.

- Use industry research, analyst reports, audits of competitors' experiences and communications, and social media listening to help you understand each brand's points of strength and differentiation.
- Synthesize your findings into a succinct description of each competitor's unique value.
- Write the name of each competitor and its unique value on an index card that can be affixed to the charts you will create in the next step. Make several copies of each card.

COMPETITORS & THEIR UNIQUE VALUE

List the major competitors in your competitive frame of reference and the unique value that each delivers.

Competitor:

Unique Value:

Transfer this list onto a series of index cards, one card for each competitor, and then make several copies of each card.

4 Draw maps.

Draw competitive landscape map charts to identify the competitive whitespace for your brand.

- Begin by drawing several large charts, each with an x and y axis.

- For the first chart, start with axes that are standard for your category -- for a snack food, for example, your axes might be low price vs. premium, sweet vs. salty, or for kids vs. for adults.

- Put the cards of the brands in your competitive frame of reference onto the map in the places that best indicate their positions relative to the axes.

- Move onto another chart, using different axes and placing the competitors on each. Consider axes that represent varying attributes for your category (for snack foods, you might think about single serve vs. multiple servings or familiar ingredients vs. new ones).

- Continue to create new charts, experimenting with different axes, especially those that speak to customer emotions (energizing vs. relaxing) or different usage occasions (meal replacement vs. treat). Also use axes that relate to your answers to #1 (what business you're in) and #2 (what lifestage you're in).

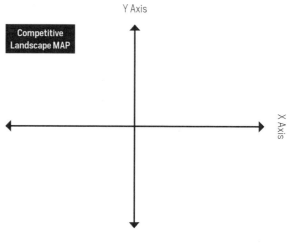

Blank Landscape Map

Example Competitive Landscape Map

5 **Evaluate opportunities.**

Finally, identify the unique value of your brand by evaluating the opportunities in the landscapes.

● For each chart, pinpoint where the competitive whitespace (e.g., unclaimed, open space) is and put a card with your brand name in that whitespace.

● Examine the positions and unique values of competitive brands on each chart and identify the potential unique value of your brand relative to theirs.

● Once you've completed and examined several charts, the one that reveals the most compelling value for your brand should become clear. It's the one with the most significant whitespace and the most differentiating benefit for your brand.

TIPS:

● This process involves both art and science -- and it takes some practice to do it well -- so, take your time to repeat parts of the process until you feel confident in the outcome.

● The most disruptive brands are the ones that introduce new category dimensions, so push yourselves to identify map axes that reveal new ways of competing in the category. For example, instead of simply using a low-price-to-high-price axis, consider an axis of standard-item-pricing-to-new-bundled-pricing.

● Although your brand might deliver value to customers in several different ways, this process should lead you to identify the primary value aspect for your brand. Then the other elements of your value should be relegated to lower priority or support status.

FRAME OF REFERENCE & UNIQUE VALUE

Write in the frame of reference for your brand here:

....

Write in the unique value of your brand here:

....

Congratulations! You're completed the step that most people find the most difficult and you're almost finished.

STEP 5: DETERMINE YOUR KEY BRAND DIFFERENTIATORS

As you scale-up your brand, the last step is to identify and develop your key brand differentiators.

WHAT IS A BRAND DIFFERENTIATOR?

Differentiation may quite possibly be the top priority in brand development. In today's competitive business environment, simply being *better* than other brands no longer creates a sustainable advantage. Your brand must be *different*. Your brand must stand out from all the other choices your customers have.

The best way to establish brand differentiation is to leverage one or more key differentiators. A brand differentiator is a unique feature or aspect of your product or service that sets it apart from competing brands. A single differentiator or a robust set of them form the basis for how you establish and maintain competitive advantage.

In the end, your key brand differentiators form the basis for the "reason(s) to believe" in the Competitive Brand Positioning statement framework:

> For [core customer], we are the [competitive frame of reference] who does [unique value], because [reason(s) to believe].

They give your brand credibility by explaining why and how your brand is able to deliver its unique value.

CLARIFY AND PRIORITIZE YOUR DIFFERENTIATORS

Sometimes your key brand differentiator(s) is obvious and definitive. If that's the case, then you can skip this step. But if you have many possible differentiators, you need to clarify and prioritize them. I recommend identifying three key differentiators and designating the lead one among the three. Here's how:

1 Make a list.

List all the things that do or could differentiate your brand – consider the following:

- **target market** -- the specific customer segment(s) your brand appeals to
- **attributes** -- descriptive qualities or characteristics of your product or service (Don't confuse these with the defining brand attributes you identified in Step 2. Attributes here are more tangible than those of your brand -- for example, your brand might be defined by its refreshing attitude, while your product might be differentiated by its fresh fruit ingredients).
- **ingredients or specifications** -- the unique elements that comprise your product
- **methods** -- the proprietary method by which your product is made or your service is delivered
- **claims** -- definitive statements that can be made about your brand
- **brand heritage and/or story** -- the narrative of why and how your brand came to exist
- **technologies and/or patents** -- specific technologies in your product or service and/or the patents you hold or have applied for
- **performance or efficacy** -- the unique way your product works or result it produces
- **endorsements** -- statements of approval or support from an influential person(s), group(s), or organization(s)
- **awards** -- recognition you've earned
- **company** -- your organization's unique programs, people, design, etc.
- **brand personality** -- the way your brand expresses itself

2 Evaluate each differentiator.

Rate each differentiator on the following dimensions, using a 1 to 5 scale where 1 = weak and 5 = strong:

- **importance to core customers** -- your differentiation must make a difference to the people you want to attract
- **difference from competitors** -- the greater the difference, the stronger the differentiator
- **ease of achieving and sustaining** -- consider how easy it is to establish and maintain the differentiation
- **relevance to brand essence/purpose** -- the strongest differentiators closely relate to or support your brand purpose

Brand differentiator	Importance to core customers	Difference from competitors	Ease of achieving and sustaining	Relevance to brand purpose
	Rate each differentiator on a scale of 1 to 5. where 1 = weak and 5 = strong.			
1.				
2.				
3.				
4.				
5.				
6.				
7.				

Brand Differentiator Evaluation Matrix Template

3 Identify the priorities.

Use the ratings to identify the top 3–4 differentiators and, of those, the lead one.

4 Translate into reason(s) to believe.

Consider how the differentiators explain, support, or even bolster the unique value of your brand that you identified in Step 5. Articulate your key differentiators in a phrase or series of bullet points that provide a reason(s) to believe your unique brand value.

KEY DIFFERENTIATORS

1. Write in your key differentiators here:

....

....

....

....

2. Place a star next to the one that is the primary differentiator.

DENISE LEE YOHN
brand-building expert | speaker | author

TIPS:

- Ensure each differentiator is clear and specific. Each should be understandable in language used by your target customers and each should be as descriptive and definitive as possible.

- If you have the resources and capabilities, consider using A/B testing among your core customer target to help you understand the relative importance of your differentiators.

Now that you've completed Steps 3 – 5, you should be able to draft your complete Competitive Brand Positioning statement.

COMPETITIVE BRAND POSITONING

Follow the framework:

For [core customer], we are the [competitive frame of reference] who does [unique value], because [reason(s) to believe].

Fill in the blanks:

For ....

we are the ....

who ....

because ....

BONUS: ASSESS YOUR BRAND POWER

As you scale-up your brand, you may want to assess the strength of your brand, so I'm including a basic 5-point brand assessment as a bonus tool.

FIVE DIMENSIONS OF BRAND POWER

This assessment covers five critical dimensions of brand power. These dimensions indicate the strength of your brand to establish and maintain competitive advantage, command a price premium, and win customers' loyalty.

These are not the only dimensions of brand power, but I've found that they are the most fundamental ones. They provide a simple way to assess your brand power.

ASSESS EARLY AND ASSESS OFTEN

You can use the brand assessment at various points in your journey:

- Before you start the work on your brand platform, use the assessment to shape your brand vision and/or to create a baseline.
- After you've completed the steps in this workbook, you can use it to see if you think you're headed in the right direction.
- As you implement your strategic brand platform, you can also use the five dimensions as filters to help you decide what to do and what not to.
- And after your platform has been in place for awhile, use the tool for periodic assessment and course correction.

This tool is a self-assessment, meaning it draws upon your own opinions. As with all self-assessments, it's best used in conjunction with research that investigates the opinions of your core customer target and other stakeholders -- e.g., partners, employees, etc.

TOOL: BRAND ASSESSMENT

For each of the following dimensions, rate your brand on a scale of 1 to 5 where 1 = Poor and 5 = Excellent.

1. Meaningful -- A meaningful brand is relevant and compelling to a valuable customer target(s). Let me break this down a bit:

- **relevant** -- Your brand should connect to a customer need or want.
- **compelling** -- Your brand should prompt action or reaction.
- **valuable customer target** -- Your brand should appeal to customers who want to buy your product/service or add value to your business in some other way.

2. Differentiating – A brand should be distinct from other options. And here's the important part, it should be distinct in a way that customers perceive is important. Your brand differentiation can't be negligible or simply a veneer.

3. Believable – Your brand should be grounded in the natural and inherent strengths of your product/service. Your brand can't just be a promise; it must be a promise delivered. A corollary is if it sounds too good to be true, it probably is. Customers must believe that you can and will deliver on your brand promise -- and sometimes you have to earn their permission to even make a claim.

4. Transcendent -- A transcendent brand conveys value beyond a specific offering. This means it connects with customers at a higher level. In my book, ***What Great Brands Do***, I write about how great brands avoid selling products. I explain that people are emotional creatures and we make purchase decisions based on our feelings. So, your brand should satisfy customers' emotional needs and/or offer access to an identity they want to experience and express.

5. Sustainable – A brand should be based on an enduring idea that enables your business to resonate and compete now and in the future. The appeal of a brand that is tied to a fad or fleeting trend is short-lived and entirely dependent upon circumstances outside your control. You should conceive of your brand to make both an immediate and a long-lasting impact.

	Circle a rating for your brand on a scale of 1 to 5, where 1 = Poor and 5 = Excellent.				
Meaningful	1	2	3	4	5
Differentiating	1	2	3	4	5
Believable	1	2	3	4	5
Transcendent	1	2	3	4	5
Sustainable	1	2.	3	4	5

Brand Assessment

ONWARD!

Great job! You've made it through all the steps to scale-up your brand. You now have the tools, methods, and information to form a strategic brand platform that will fuel your growth and inform your evolution.

Put the results of all your work together in a one-pager:

BRAND IDENTITY		
PURPOSE	VALUES	DEFINING ATTRIBUTES

COMPETITIVE BRAND POSITIONING	
CORE CUSTOMER TARGET	FRAME OF REFERENCE
UNIQUE VALUE	KEY DIFFERENTIATORS

Strategic Brand Platform Template

mail@deniseleeyohn.com || http://deniseleeyohn.com
© 2016 Denise Lee Yohn, Inc. All Rights Reserved.

DENISE LEE YOHN
brand-building expert | speaker | author

WHAT'S NEXT?!

Although you've just completed the most important part of your journey to a scaled brand, it's really only the first step. You now need to use your strategic brand platform to drive, align, and guide everything your company does. Use your strategic brand platform to:

- **Cultivate a strong brand-led culture inside your organization,** by using it to guide your hiring, training, and employee experience
- **Make strategic decisions** about what to do and what not to do
- **Design and run your operations** on a day to day basis
- **Create extraordinary customer experiences,** by ensuring every aspect of every customer touchpoint is on-brand

Don't let your brand strategy remain words on a page. Ensure everyone who works on your brand understands it, embraces it, and uses it in their daily decision-making and actions.

Your brand is not what you *say* you are – it's what you *do*.

WANT MORE?

If you're looking for more helpful resources, check out:

DENISE'S BESTSELLING BOOK:

What Great Brands Do: The Seven Brand-Building Principles That Separate the Best from the Rest (Jossey-Bass)

Packed with insightful case studies from companies like Starbucks, GE, and IKEA, *What Great Brands Do* explains how top companies develop standout brands that foster customer loyalty and increase profit margins. Brand-building expert Denise Lee Yohn translates these studies into actionable guidelines by sharing the seven major principles that are essential for brand excellence. Get your copy and start learning how to use your brand not just to gain a competitive edge, but to change the game completely.

Available in hardcover, e-book, and audio book.

DENISE'S LATEST E-BOOK:

Extraordinary Experiences: What Great Retail and Restaurant Brands Do

How do some stores and restaurants break through the clutter; compete with bigger, online competitors; and manage to grow and thrive when so many others fail? They earn customer love and loyalty by creatively designing and consistently delivering great retail customer experiences. Packed with compelling stories and practical principles, *Extraordinary Experiences* is the brand-building and retail customer experience bible on every business leader's shelf.

DENISE'S NEWSLETTER:

Get regular briefings about brands and brand-building and how to build a strong, valuable, sustaining brand from Denise -- delivered right to your in-box. Sign up now!
(http://deniseleeyohn.com/newseltter)

ABOUT DENISE

Denise Lee Yohn is the go-to expert on brand-building for national media outlets, an in-demand speaker and consultant, and an influential writer.

News media including FOX Business TV, CNBC, The Wall Street Journal, and The New York Times call on Denise when they want an expert point-of-view on hot business issues. Denise enjoys challenging readers to think differently about brand-building in her regular contributions to Harvard Business Review and Forbes.

With her expertise and personal approach, Denise has become a popular keynote speaker, addressing business leaders around the world.

Denise initially cultivated her brand-building approaches through several high-level positions in advertising and client-side marketing. Consulting clients have included Target, Oakley, Dunkin' Donuts, and other leading companies.

Contact Denise to book her to inspire and teach your organization.
(http://deniseleeyohn.com/contact)

DENISE LEE YOHN
brand-building expert | speaker | author